MAD LIBS ☺ JUNIOR™

SUMMER FUN MAD LIBS JUNIOR

By Roger Price and Leonard Stern

Mad Libs
An Imprint of Penguin Random House

MAD LIBS
Penguin Young Readers Group
An Imprint of Penguin Random House LLC

Mad Libs format and text copyright © 2004 by Penguin Random House LLC. All rights reserved.

Concept created by Roger Price & Leonard Stern

Published by Mad Libs,
an imprint of Penguin Random House LLC,
345 Hudson Street, New York, New York 10014.
Printed in the USA.

ISBN 9780843107593
21

**MAD LIBS JUNIOR™ is a game for kids who don't like games!
It can be played by one, two, three, four, or forty.**

RIDICULOUSLY SIMPLE DIRECTIONS:
At the top of each page in this book, you will find four columns of words, each headed by a symbol. Each symbol represents a part of speech. The symbols are:

★   ☺   →   ?
NOUNS   ADJECTIVES   VERBS   MISC.

MAD LIBS JUNIOR™ is fun to play with friends, but you can also play it by yourself! To begin, look at the story on the page below. When you come to a blank space in the story, look at the symbol that appears underneath. Then find the same symbol on this page and pick a word that appears below the symbol. Put that word in the blank space, and cross out the word, so you don't use it again. Continue doing this throughout the story until you've filled in all the spaces. Finally, read your story aloud and laugh!

EXAMPLE:

"Good-bye!" he said, as he jumped into his _____ and _____
                             ?   →

off with his pet _____ .
                      ★

★ NOUNS	☺ ADJECTIVES	→ VERBS	? MISC.
hamster	curly	drove	car
dog	purple	~~danced~~	boat
cat	wet	drank	roller-skate
~~giraffe~~	tired	twirled	taxicab
monkey	silly	swam	~~surfboard~~

"Good-bye!" he said, as he jumped into his __SURFBOARD__ and __DANCED__
                                  ?   →

off with his pet __GIRAFFE__ .
                    ★

In case you haven't learned about the parts of speech yet, here is a quick lesson:

A **NOUN** ★ is the name of a person, place, or thing. *Sidewalk, umbrella, bathtub,* and *roller blades* are nouns.

An **ADJECTIVE** ☺ describes a person, place, or thing. *Lumpy, soft, ugly, messy,* and *short* are adjectives.

A **VERB** ➜ is an action word. *Run, jump,* and *swim* are verbs.

MISC. ? will be any word that does not apply to the other categories. Some examples of a word that could be miscellaneous are: *part of the body, animal, number, color,* and *a place.*

MAD LIBS JUNIOR™ is fun to play with friends, but you can also play it by yourself! To begin, look at the story on the page below. When you come to a blank space in the story, look at the symbol that appears underneath. Then find the same symbol on this page and pick a word that appears below the symbol. Put that word in the blank space, and cross out the word, so you don't use it again. Continue doing this throughout the story until you've filled in all the spaces. Finally, read your story aloud and laugh!

A DAY AT THE POOL

★	☺	→	?
NOUNS	**ADJECTIVES**	**VERBS**	**MISC.**
grown-ups	stupid	bite	2
nachos	wet	jump	15
monkeys	slippery	kick	7
friends	sunny	dance	800
ice pops	lazy	beg	5
elves	hairy	sniff	12
hot dogs	ugly	slide	6
toilets	rainy	cry	2,000
basketballs	smelly	scream	8
sharks	chunky	dive	24
cheese puffs	muddy	wiggle	9
pencils	boring	slip	13

MAD LIBS JUNIOR
A DAY AT THE POOL

My favorite thing to do during the summertime is to spend a/an

_____ day at the pool. My mom drops me off at

_____ o'clock and doesn't pick me up again until

_____ . It's great! _____ and

Minnows is one of our favorite pool games. We also love to

_____ for pennies and play Marco Polo. I hate

when the lifeguards _____ into their whistles and

announce "_____ swim." This is when all the kids

have to get out of the pool and only the _____

are allowed to swim. It lasts for _____ minutes!

To pass the time, I go to the snack bar and buy some yummy

_____ —sometimes I even share!

MAD LIBS JUNIOR™ is fun to play with friends, but you can also play it by yourself! To begin, look at the story on the page below. When you come to a blank space in the story, look at the symbol that appears underneath. Then find the same symbol on this page and pick a word that appears below the symbol. Put that word in the blank space, and cross out the word, so you don't use it again. Continue doing this throughout the story until you've filled in all the spaces. Finally, read your story aloud and laugh!

MY FIRST PLANE TRIP

★ NOUNS	☺ ADJECTIVES	➡ VERBS	? MISC.
sausage	nasty	giggle	75
windmill	crispy	barf	3
toothbrush	smart	sing	9
octopus	ugly	shake	767
magazine	tasty	cry	92
pickle	cheap	squirm	11
pin	pretty	sleep	15
suitcase	stinky	juggle	1
hippo	delightful	eat	3,000
banana	furry	sweat	34
diamond	happy	jump	19
lollipop	yucky	dance	4 billion

I will never forget my very first trip on an airplane. I was

_____ years old and my family was going to Florida.
?

I was a little _____, but my dad said that I should try
☺

not to _____. When we boarded, the inside looked
➡

like a huge _____. There were rows and rows of
★

_____ seats. Each seat had a little tray and a
☺

compartment to store a/an _____. My parents let
★

me sit by the window so I could _____ during
➡

the flight. The flight attendant brought us all sodas and a/an

_____ snack. And before we landed, she gave me a little
☺

_____ with wings on it that I could pin to my
★

shirt, for being such a/an _____ passenger!
☺

MAD LIBS JUNIOR™ is fun to play with friends, but you can also play it by yourself! To begin, look at the story on the page below. When you come to a blank space in the story, look at the symbol that appears underneath. Then find the same symbol on this page and pick a word that appears below the symbol. Put that word in the blank space, and cross out the word, so you don't use it again. Continue doing this throughout the story until you've filled in all the spaces. Finally, read your story aloud and laugh!

OCEAN LAND ADVENTURE

★	😊	→	?
NOUNS	ADJECTIVES	VERBS	MISC.
T-shirt	floppy	dine	2
squid	fuzzy	dance	5,000
clown	blue	sing	50
mug	pointy	swim	6
clam	dumb	dive	20
watermelon	silky	talk	7
golf ball	funky	ski	33
cupcake	fun	leap	600
tissue	lame	play	1 million
pen	silly	surf	15
cabbage	scary	juggle	4
notepad	awesome	cook	17

MAD LIBS JUNIOR
OCEAN LAND ADVENTURE

This summer my family went on a/an _____ trip to

Ocean Land—the world's largest sea park! The mascot of Ocean

Land is a giant _____ named Squishy who likes to

_____ with all the creatures of the sea. Squishy

wears a large _____ hat and walks around all

day. For _____ dollars, you can have a/an _____

picture taken with him. Ocean Land has lots of _____

shows. My favorite was one where _____ killer

whales jumped through many flaming hoops and over a giant

_____. Then they called someone from the audience

to _____ with some dolphins. Just my luck, they

picked the _____ sitting next to me.

MAD LIBS JUNIOR™ is fun to play with friends, but you can also play it by yourself! To begin, look at the story on the page below. When you come to a blank space in the story, look at the symbol that appears underneath. Then find the same symbol on this page and pick a word that appears below the symbol. Put that word in the blank space, and cross out the word, so you don't use it again. Continue doing this throughout the story until you've filled in all the spaces. Finally, read your story aloud and laugh!

LEMONADE STAND

★ NOUNS	☺ ADJECTIVES	→ VERBS	? MISC.
tree	cold	kiss	100
peach	happy	eat	2
egg	hairy	tickle	4,000
shoe	hot	lick	89
pancake	blue	shake	32
octopus	nasty	kick	1 million
car	sad	squeeze	900
box	stupid	rub	14
wig	gross	wiggle	500
hamburger	yummy	squish	6
shirt	slimy	wash	59
toilet	horrible	bite	10,000

One _____ summer day, my sister and I were sitting

around feeling _____. We decided to make a

lemonade stand out of an old _____ in the garage.

To make the lemonade, we had to _____ about

_____ fresh lemons. Then we added a/an

_____ for flavor and _____ cups of

sugar. Our first customer was our _____ neighbor

Mr. Green, who had just finished washing his big _____.

He took one little sip and started to _____ his lips.

"Mmmm," he said. "That's one _____ glass of

lemonade!" Having a lemonade stand sure was _____ ,

and the best part was we made _____ dollars!

MAD LIBS JUNIOR™ is fun to play with friends, but you can also play it by yourself! To begin, look at the story on the page below. When you come to a blank space in the story, look at the symbol that appears underneath. Then find the same symbol on this page and pick a word that appears below the symbol. Put that word in the blank space, and cross out the word, so you don't use it again. Continue doing this throughout the story until you've filled in all the spaces. Finally, read your story aloud and laugh!

FAMILY COOKOUT

★ NOUNS	😊 ADJECTIVES	➡ VERBS	? MISC.
frog	slimy	hug	300
turtle	warty	punch	2,000
chicken	chubby	tickle	25
sweet potato	lumpy	pinch	4
fish	hairy	kiss	18
pickle	chunky	squeeze	750
ice cream	furry	poke	8,000
squid	stinky	kick	98
onion	goofy	bite	117
bubble gum	dumb	sniff	6
marshmallow	messy	lick	50
dog	gross	taste	2 million

MAD LIBS JUNIOR
FAMILY COOKOUT

Every summer my family has a/an _____ cookout.

Over _____ family members meet up. My Aunt

Trudy always tries to give me a big _____ kiss and a/an

_____ on my _____. Then there's

my cousin Freddy, who I call "Freddy the _____"

because he's so _____. My grandpa always works

the grill. He wears a big _____ hat and a silly apron

that says, "Please _____ the cook." Every year

there is a big contest to see who can make the very best

_____ pie. My great grandma always wins, even

though her pie is _____. I think everyone just lets

her win because she's _____ years old!

MAD LIBS JUNIOR™ is fun to play with friends, but you can also play it by yourself! To begin, look at the story on the page below. When you come to a blank space in the story, look at the symbol that appears underneath. Then find the same symbol on this page and pick a word that appears below the symbol. Put that word in the blank space, and cross out the word, so you don't use it again. Continue doing this throughout the story until you've filled in all the spaces. Finally, read your story aloud and laugh!

WET AND _____ WATER PARK

★ NOUNS	☺ ADJECTIVES	→ VERBS	? MISC.
toilet	fun	float	10
alligator	stupid	shoot	200
apple	slippery	swim	45
snake	giant	squirt	2
toothpick	plastic	ride	75
turnip	purple	fall	800
spider	boring	fly	10,000
snail	hairy	swim	156
carrot	rubbery	blast	3 billion
snowflake	spiky	ooze	5,000
teacup	dry	jet	99
feather	slimy	trickle	17

MAD LIBS JUNIOR

WET AND _____ WATER PARK

I love when my family goes to the water park in the summer! It's so

_____. There are over _____

different waterslides to ride. My favorite is called the Amazon

_____. It's shaped like a giant _____

and it has lots of _____ tunnels that you can

_____ through. It's so _____

that it takes _____ minutes to reach the end.

I also like _____ Falls, where you sit on a rubber

_____ and _____ through the

water until you reach the _____ waterfall at the

end. There is also a huge _____ pool!

MAD LIBS JUNIOR™ is fun to play with friends, but you can also play it by yourself! To begin, look at the story on the page below. When you come to a blank space in the story, look at the symbol that appears underneath. Then find the same symbol on this page and pick a word that appears below the symbol. Put that word in the blank space, and cross out the word, so you don't use it again. Continue doing this throughout the story until you've filled in all the spaces. Finally, read your story aloud and laugh!

SCOUTS CAMPING TRIP

★ NOUNS	☺ ADJECTIVES	➡ VERBS	? MISC.
meat loaf	scratchy	swimming	12
blanket	ugly	burping	4
flower	wild	singing	200
wolf	hot	cooking	2
sweater	fuzzy	dancing	65
onion	cold	crying	43
teddy bear	scaly	farting	4 billion
raccoon	hairy	sewing	7
French fry	smelly	fighting	365
sausage	soft	screaming	52
beaver	squishy	shivering	500
snake	mean	whining	3

MAD LIBS JUNIOR
SCOUTS CAMPING TRIP

This summer I went on a _____ -day camping trip with

?

my _____ Scout troop. This was my big chance to

★

earn my _____ badge. Camping was really

➡

_____ at first. For dinner, we each roasted a/an

☺

_____ on a stick over the camp fire. After dinner we

★

all started _____ and telling scary _____

➡   ★

stories. Finally we crawled in our _____ tents and

☺

went to bed. After _____ days of camping, I smelled

?

like a/an _____ and I wanted to go home. The

★

only badge I got was for _____ !

➡

MAD LIBS JUNIOR™ is fun to play with friends, but you can also play it by yourself! To begin, look at the story on the page below. When you come to a blank space in the story, look at the symbol that appears underneath. Then find the same symbol on this page and pick a word that appears below the symbol. Put that word in the blank space, and cross out the word, so you don't use it again. Continue doing this throughout the story until you've filled in all the spaces. Finally, read your story aloud and laugh!

ISLAND CRUISE

★   😀   ➡   ?

NOUNS	ADJECTIVES	VERBS	MISC.
octopus	smelly	burping	37
pickle	ugly	swimming	400
monkey	awesome	dancing	15
milkshake	weird	screaming	72
unicorn	stupid	jumping	7,000
flamingo	cool	eating	85
lobster	boring	farting	9
pirate	lame	yelling	230
umbrella	funny	staring	3
parrot	scary	biting	950
whale	wild	clapping	20
donut	bumpy	sneezing	11

MAD LIBS JUNIOR

ISLAND CRUISE

Last summer, my grandparents took us on a/an _____

cruise around the _____ Islands. The cruise ship

was really _____. It even had _____

swimming pools! My dad liked that you could eat _____

times a day. I think he gained about _____ pounds!

Every day we stopped at some _____ island, where

everyone would start _____. One time we went

snorkeling and I saw a/an _____ and a great white

_____! At night on the ship there were lots of

_____ things to do. On our last night, they had a/an

_____ contest and my mom won—the prize was a

free _____ for the whole family!

MAD LIBS JUNIOR™ is fun to play with friends, but you can also play it by yourself! To begin, look at the story on the page below. When you come to a blank space in the story, look at the symbol that appears underneath. Then find the same symbol on this page and pick a word that appears below the symbol. Put that word in the blank space, and cross out the word, so you don't use it again. Continue doing this throughout the story until you've filled in all the spaces. Finally, read your story aloud and laugh!

AMUSEMENT PARK

★ NOUNS	😊 ADJECTIVES	➡ VERBS	? MISC.
kangaroo	dumb	scream	2
fig	sick	dance	2,000
dragon	bumpy	barf	50
fish	hairy	laugh	9
snail	slimy	burp	300
funhouse	yucky	cry	78
donkey	smelly	sing	16
gumdrop	crazy	jump	430
peanut	healthy	squirm	13
squash	scary	climb	92
spider	smart	yell	5
cat	tasty	pop	22

Every summer my mom gets us a _____ -day pass to
?

our favorite amusement park,_____ Kingdom! My
★

favorite ride is the Flying _____. It spins around
★

until you feel like you want to _____. One time we
➡

rode it _____ times in a row. My sister felt a little too
?

_____, so we had to stop. Her favorite ride is the
☺

Screaming _____ roller coaster. It has _____
★   **?**

loops and a dark _____tunnel! We always get
☺

_____ after riding the rides. Mom gives us
☺

_____ dollars to spend on a _____
?   ☺

lunch, but we always spend it on a chocolate-dipped

_____ instead!
★

MAD LIBS JUNIOR™ is fun to play with friends, but you can also play it by yourself! To begin, look at the story on the page below. When you come to a blank space in the story, look at the symbol that appears underneath. Then find the same symbol on this page and pick a word that appears below the symbol. Put that word in the blank space, and cross out the word, so you don't use it again. Continue doing this throughout the story until you've filled in all the spaces. Finally, read your story aloud and laugh!

MINIATURE GOLF

★ NOUNS	☺ ADJECTIVES	➡ VERBS	? MISC.
giraffe	green	crawl	12
bear	lumpy	run	4
pirate	square	wiggle	200
dinosaur	stupid	limbo	2
bagel	slimy	fall	65
toothbrush	cheap	dance	43
pencil	smelly	roll	4 billion
penguin	wooden	swim	7
tulip	silly	jump	365
flea	shiny	giggle	52
banana	stinky	dive	500
toaster	funny	shimmy	3

Every Friday night, my friends and I go to Big _____

Pete's Mini Golf. There are _____ holes and you get

?

_____ strokes to get the ball in the hole. I always

?

pick a _____ ball, for good luck. I like to use a

_____ putter that's about the size of a

_____. All of the holes have really _____

★

decorations. The 9ᵗʰ is my favorite. It has a _____-

?

foot-tall _____ with big _____

★

legs that you have to _____ under. One time it took

➡

me _____ minutes to do it. The 18ᵗʰ hole has a big

?

_____ windmill. If you can make your ball

_____, you win a free _____

➡   ★

and get your picture taken with Pete!

MAD LIBS JUNIOR™ is fun to play with friends, but you can also play it by yourself! To begin, look at the story on the page below. When you come to a blank space in the story, look at the symbol that appears underneath. Then find the same symbol on this page and pick a word that appears below the symbol. Put that word in the blank space, and cross out the word, so you don't use it again. Continue doing this throughout the story until you've filled in all the spaces. Finally, read your story aloud and laugh!

SWIMMING LESSONS

★ NOUNS	☺ ADJECTIVES	→ VERBS	? MISC.
poodle	slippery	wiggle	5
goldfish	wet	swim	20
turkey	hard	bark	18
monkey	gross	shake	32
noodle	silly	dive	500
dolphin	boring	jump	2
duck	tough	screech	75
sausage	lovely	kick	3,000
brick	nasty	crawl	99
seal	warm	splash	7
goat	fun	stroke	10
hippo	slimy	float	900

MAD LIBS JUNIOR
SWIMMING LESSONS

At the beginning of the summer, the only stroke I could do was the

_____ paddle. Mom said I had to learn to _____ ★ ➡

in the water without holding my _____. She signed ★

me up for _____ weeks of swimming lessons. The ?

instructor was a very _____-looking lady who ☺

made me jump in the water and _____ like a/an ➡

_____. I had to _____ all the ★ ➡

way down the length of the pool _____ times and ?

could only take _____ breaths. Finally, I had to tread ?

water for _____ minutes. Now I can swim like a/an ?

_____, but I still like floating around on my ★

blow-up _____ more! ★

MAD LIBS JUNIOR™ is fun to play with friends, but you can also play it by yourself! To begin, look at the story on the page below. When you come to a blank space in the story, look at the symbol that appears underneath. Then find the same symbol on this page and pick a word that appears below the symbol. Put that word in the blank space, and cross out the word, so you don't use it again. Continue doing this throughout the story until you've filled in all the spaces. Finally, read your story aloud and laugh!

BUG HUNTING

★ NOUNS	😊 ADJECTIVES	➡ VERBS	? MISC.
dog	floppy	swinging	12
lady	scary	hopping	5
elephant	hairy	shaking	200
lion	blue	twirling	19
baby	slimy	falling	76
snowman	fun	singing	40
tiger	silly	crying	3
giraffe	dumb	screeching	9
clown	nasty	dancing	89
camel	shiny	jumping	4,000
zebra	wild	laughing	56
monster	friendly	clapping	33

Bug hunting is a _____ thing to do on warm

summer days. I shove a/an _____ into my backpack,

grab my net, and head off to the _____ backyard.

One day I caught a bug with _____ legs and two

_____ wings. My field guide said it was called

a/an "_____ beetle." They can grow up to

_____ inches long! Just then, I heard something

_____ in the bushes, so I started _____ with

my net. Whatever it was, it was really _____! I

looked in the net and I saw a huge _____ with

big _____ eyes. I never caught one of those before!

MAD LIBS JUNIOR™ is fun to play with friends, but you can also play it by yourself! To begin, look at the story on the page below. When you come to a blank space in the story, look at the symbol that appears underneath. Then find the same symbol on this page and pick a word that appears below the symbol. Put that word in the blank space, and cross out the word, so you don't use it again. Continue doing this throughout the story until you've filled in all the spaces. Finally, read your story aloud and laugh!

DUDE RANCH

★ NOUNS	☺ ADJECTIVES	➡ VERBS	? MISC.
cornflakes	stupid	sing	5
lizards	furry	giggle	45
strawberries	slimy	burp	16
chipmunks	curly	run	200
mushrooms	shiny	yell	70
squirrels	grisly	dance	13
jellyfish	scary	laugh	30
turkeys	perky	snort	22
turnips	ugly	spit	99
cream puffs	crusty	gallop	6
hot dogs	wild	swim	3,000
chickens	stinky	sew	8

MAD LIBS JUNIOR.
DUDE RANCH

My dad and I went to a dude ranch for _____ days. I
                                              ?

wanted to learn to _____ just like a cowboy. Our
                          ➡

guide was a/an _____ cowboy who wore cool boots,
                      😊

a/an _____ -gallon hat, and a big _____
          ?   😊

belt buckle. He greeted us, "Howdy _____!" and told
                                              ⭐

us we could call him by his nickname, _____. He
                                              😊

taught us to herd wild _____ with lassoes. My dad
                              ⭐

even roped a huge bull with _____ sharp horns. The
                                  ?

bull saw my dad and started to _____, but my dad
                                        ➡

wasn't scared! At night we'd sit around the fire eating _____
                                                              ⭐

and potatoes, listening to stories of _____ from the
                                              ⭐

good old days in the _____ West. I sure will miss the
                            😊

dude ranch!

MAD LIBS JUNIOR™ is fun to play with friends, but you can also play it by yourself! To begin, look at the story on the page below. When you come to a blank space in the story, look at the symbol that appears underneath. Then find the same symbol on this page and pick a word that appears below the symbol. Put that word in the blank space, and cross out the word, so you don't use it again. Continue doing this throughout the story until you've filled in all the spaces. Finally, read your story aloud and laugh!

GOING TO LONDON

★ NOUNS	☺ ADJECTIVES	➡ VERBS	? MISC.
cupcakes	slimy	laugh	2
goldfish	nasty	dance	300
poodles	dumb	shout	2 million
sandwiches	crunchy	sing	15
skateboards	silly	giggle	7
hippos	shiny	scream	85
pickles	pointy	cry	50
hamburgers	fancy	smell	100
snails	smelly	run	9
pigeons	greasy	jump	5,000
sausages	brown	wiggle	650
cakes	goofy	skip	17

MAD LIBS JUNIOR
GOING TO LONDON

Next summer my whole family is going to _____ in

London. I hear they have giant double-decker _____

that you can ride around the city on. My mom wants to see

_____ Ben, a big _____ clock

in the middle of the city that starts to _____ every

hour. We're also going to Buckingham Palace, the _____

mansion where the queen and her _____ live. Dad

wants to see the collection of crown _____. They're

worth over _____ dollars! I can't wait to eat some

_____ and chips—a/an _____

English meal. I'd better pack some _____ for the

plane ride. It will take _____ hours to get there!

MAD LIBS JUNIOR™ is fun to play with friends, but you can also play it by yourself! To begin, look at the story on the page below. When you come to a blank space in the story, look at the symbol that appears underneath. Then find the same symbol on this page and pick a word that appears below the symbol. Put that word in the blank space, and cross out the word, so you don't use it again. Continue doing this throughout the story until you've filled in all the spaces. Finally, read your story aloud and laugh!

HOW TO SURVIVE A FAMILY ROAD TRIP

★ NOUNS	☺ ADJECTIVES	→ VERBS	? MISC.
truck	bad	tickle	3
goat	stupid	pinch	200
mustache	silly	poke	10
elephant	nasty	kick	75
snake	funny	sniff	800
horse	goofy	lick	450
duck	loud	bite	17
van	annoying	hug	11
pumpkin	dumb	squeeze	4 billion
bed	crazy	shake	5
rooster	lame	kiss	9,000
helicopter	stinky	smack	26

MAD LIBS JUNIOR

HOW TO SURVIVE A FAMILY ROAD TRIP

- Make up a/an _____ game to play in the car—like

the one where you _____ each other every time

you see a/an _____ go by.

- Make sure to go to the bathroom at every _____

rest stop. That way your parents won't have to stop the car every

_____ minutes.

- Have a sing-along with fun songs like "The Wheels on

the _____," "Mary Had a Little _____,"

and "_____ Bottles of Juice on the Wall." (Try not

to complain about your dad's _____ voice!)

- Don't do any _____ thing that makes your mom

scream, "Don't make me come back there and _____ you!"

MAD LIBS JUNIOR™ is fun to play with friends, but you can also play it by yourself! To begin, look at the story on the page below. When you come to a blank space in the story, look at the symbol that appears underneath. Then find the same symbol on this page and pick a word that appears below the symbol. Put that word in the blank space, and cross out the word, so you don't use it again. Continue doing this throughout the story until you've filled in all the spaces. Finally, read your story aloud and laugh!

GRAND CANYON

★ NOUNS	☺ ADJECTIVES	➡ VERBS	? MISC.
donut	stupid	yell	3
armadillo	wet	burp	500
potato	slippery	sing	9,000
bowl	sunny	fart	64
egg	lazy	hiccup	5
taco	hairy	cough	3 million
football	ugly	scream	10
submarine	rainy	laugh	2
pumpkin	smelly	yelp	75
spaceship	chunky	cry	16
cupcake	muddy	giggle	90
tomato	boring	clap	30

MAD LIBS ☺ JUNIOR

GRAND CANYON

Every summer my family goes to a different _____ ☺

park. We've been to _____ so far! We all love to

_____ in the great outdoors. This year we went to

Grand Canyon Park. It's a _____ -foot rocky hole in

Arizona. It's shaped like a huge _____ . Some people

think it was formed when a giant _____ crashed

into the Earth _____ years ago. We rode down the

canyon on the back of some _____ mules. Then we

took a ride in a big rubber _____ down the

Colorado River. The coolest thing about the canyon is if you

_____ into it loudly, you can hear the echo

_____ times!

MAD LIBS JUNIOR™ is fun to play with friends, but you can also play it by yourself! To begin, look at the story on the page below. When you come to a blank space in the story, look at the symbol that appears underneath. Then find the same symbol on this page and pick a word that appears below the symbol. Put that word in the blank space, and cross out the word, so you don't use it again. Continue doing this throughout the story until you've filled in all the spaces. Finally, read your story aloud and laugh!

5 STEPS TO PACKING YOUR SUITCASE

★ NOUNS	☺ ADJECTIVES	➡ VERBS	? MISC.
banana	dirty	jump	5
turkey	sunny	run	400
sock	furry	eat	99
cabbage	cold	dive	75
bag	smelly	skip	15
coconut	silly	dance	8
lunchbox	slimy	fart	2,000
teddy bear	funny	cry	300
puppet	stupid	sneeze	47
tomato	ugly	leap	10
donut	warm	swim	3
monkey	bad	wiggle	2 billion

MAD LIBS JUNIOR

5 STEPS TO PACKING YOUR SUITCASE

- Always take lots of _____ underwear. It's good to

  have at least _____ pairs.

- Bring your favorite blanket and stuffed _____ to sleep

  with. That way you won't get _____ while you are away.

- Don't forget to take your _____ brush and use it

  at least _____ times a day.

- Pack some playing cards in your _____. That way,

  you can play "Go _____" or "Old _____"

  on the plane or in the car.

- If you are going somewhere _____ that has a swimming

  pool, remember to take your _____. No one likes

  to _____ in the nude!

MAD LIBS JUNIOR™ is fun to play with friends, but you can also play it by yourself! To begin, look at the story on the page below. When you come to a blank space in the story, look at the symbol that appears underneath. Then find the same symbol on this page and pick a word that appears below the symbol. Put that word in the blank space, and cross out the word, so you don't use it again. Continue doing this throughout the story until you've filled in all the spaces. Finally, read your story aloud and laugh!

LIFE AT THE BEACH

★	☺	➡	?
NOUNS	ADJECTIVES	VERBS	MISC.
cat	smelly	sleep	3
ice cube	scary	dance	20
beet	stupid	burp	500
shrimp	purple	eat	17
lemon	crazy	jump	92
dragon	wooden	read	12
hat	round	bathe	5
jellyfish	green	dive	24
foot	yucky	skip	3,000
whale	ugly	fall	36
sailboat	bright	laugh	11
seashell	shiny	sit	83

MAD LIBS JUNIOR

LIFE AT THE BEACH

Every summer my family rents an old _____ beach

house and spends a week of _____ family time

together. One time I dangled a/an _____ in the

water and caught a/an _____ -foot-long

_____ . It had _____ eyes and a

big _____ on its back. After that I was scared to

_____ in the water for a month! My mom sunbathes

for _____ hours a day. After two days, she's as

_____ as a/an _____ . For the

rest of the trip, she has to keep a/an _____ on her head

to stay cool. My _____ little brother lets me bury him up

to his _____ in the sand. I say I'll come back in

_____ minutes, but I never do!

MAD LIBS JUNIOR™ is fun to play with friends, but you can also play it by yourself! To begin, look at the story on the page below. When you come to a blank space in the story, look at the symbol that appears underneath. Then find the same symbol on this page and pick a word that appears below the symbol. Put that word in the blank space, and cross out the word, so you don't use it again. Continue doing this throughout the story until you've filled in all the spaces. Finally, read your story aloud and laugh!

LETTER FROM CAMP

★ NOUNS	☺ ADJECTIVES	→ VERBS	? MISC.
snail	dirty	crying	2
spider	sunny	wiggling	365
wolf	furry	eating	40
ant	cold	farting	10
ladybug	smelly	falling	29
dinosaur	silly	dancing	13
turtle	slimy	cheating	200
bear	funny	burping	3
snake	stupid	stinking	56
flea	ugly	sleeping	9
octopus	warm	screaming	80
tick	bad	staring	14

MAD LIBS ✪ JUNIOR
LETTER FROM CAMP

Dear Mom and Dad,

Thanks for sending me to Camp _____ ★ this summer!

The good news is I won the camp _____ ➡ contest.

The bad news is I was bitten by a giant _____ ★. My

leg was _____ 😊 and swollen all day. The food is really

_____ 😊. Last night I ate something that looked like a/an

_____ ★ covered with gravy. It tasted pretty _____ 😊!

See you in _____ ❓ days! I can't wait.

Your _____ 😊 son,

Sam

P.S. My counselor says if I don't stop _____ ➡ so much

I'll have to go home!

MAD LIBS JUNIOR™ is fun to play with friends, but you can also play it by yourself! To begin, look at the story on the page below. When you come to a blank space in the story, look at the symbol that appears underneath. Then find the same symbol on this page and pick a word that appears below the symbol. Put that word in the blank space, and cross out the word, so you don't use it again. Continue doing this throughout the story until you've filled in all the spaces. Finally, read your story aloud and laugh!

NEW YORK CITY

★	☺	➡	?
NOUNS	**ADJECTIVES**	**VERBS**	**MISC.**
banana	stinky	sing	15
mug	brown	dance	2
sweatshirt	rotten	juggle	9
pickle	cool	sneeze	78
teddy bear	dirty	eat	5,000
key chain	shiny	sleep	10
pineapple	silly	run	3
dog	stolen	jump	45
ape	fresh	fart	20
pancake	smelly	burp	12
hat	shiny	giggle	6
parrot	funny	swim	99

MAD LIBS ⊙ JUNIOR.
NEW YORK CITY

Last week, my choir group went on a _____ -day trip to
?

New York City. I was so excited that I couldn't even _____ !
➡

We raised money for the trip by selling _____ fruit
😊

to senior citizens. New York is called "The Big _____ "
★

and there are tons of _____ things to see and do
😊

there. First my friend wanted to _____ on the
➡

_____ subway. Then we went up the Empire State
😊

Building—it's _____ floors tall! After that, we ate
?

about _____ hot dogs and a couple of those big
?

_____ pretzels. For a souvenir, I bought a/an
😊

_____ that said "I Love New York!"
★

MAD LIBS JUNIOR™ is fun to play with friends, but you can also play it by yourself! To begin, look at the story on the page below. When you come to a blank space in the story, look at the symbol that appears underneath. Then find the same symbol on this page and pick a word that appears below the symbol. Put that word in the blank space, and cross out the word, so you don't use it again. Continue doing this throughout the story until you've filled in all the spaces. Finally, read your story aloud and laugh!

A VISIT TO GRANDPA'S

★ NOUNS	☺ ADJECTIVES	➡ VERBS	? MISC.
monkey	skinny	driving	900
fiddle	fit	fishing	92
slug	ugly	swimming	50
toothpick	silly	surfing	89
bird	fat	dancing	79
clam	shiny	sailing	2,000
hippo	happy	laughing	1 million
whale	funny	floating	16
pony	goofy	jumping	200
monster	smooth	bathing	80
dolphin	sweaty	burping	400
elf	lively	splashing	99

MAD LIBS ☺ JUNIOR

A VISIT TO GRANDPA'S

Every summer I go to visit my _____ grandpa who ☺

lives in Florida. He's _____ years old, but he's as **?**

_____ as a/an _____ . Grandpa ☺ ★

always spoils me. Once he gave me a pet _____ , even ★

though mom said I couldn't have one. And he always lets me spend

_____ cents on candy when we go to the store. **?**

Grandpa drives a big _____ car and we like to go ☺

_____ down at the ocean. One time we saw a/an ➡

_____ that was _____ out in ★ ➡

the water. Grandpa and I always have _____ ☺

adventures together!

Download Mad Libs today!

Join the millions of Mad Libs fans
creating wacky and wonderful
stories on our apps!